T0196919

CAPTIVATING WORDS OF
LOVE

CAPTIVATING WORDS OF LOVE

emotional and thought provoking

Ezell Blues

CAPTIVATING WORDS OF LOVE
EMOTIONAL AND THOUGHT PROVOKING

iUniverse books may be ordered through booksellers or by contacting:

iUniverse
1663 Liberty Drive
Bloomington, IN 47403
www.iuniverse.com
1-800-Authors (1-800-288-4677)

ISBN: 978-1-5320-8772-1 (sc)
ISBN: 978-1-5320-8774-5 (hc)
ISBN: 978-1-5320-8773-8 (e)

Library of Congress Control Number: 2019917866

Print information available on the last page.

iUniverse rev. date: 02/11/2020

CONTENTS

PREFACE

The year is 2020 and the world around us has changed. A spiritual awakening of our inner divine nature is a must in strengthening us on our journey towards eternity. As I continue to evolve in my spiritual growth and into manhood, I have developed a passion for writing.

Greetings to all my family my friends and future friends.

First, I would like to thank God for creating the wonders of the universe... thank him for his endless blessings eager to impart his gifts to each of us. Key to apprehending this universal illumination is to have a greater knowledge of our true nature. My desire for you in writing "Captivating Words of Love"...is to bring healing and excitement to your heart; to captivate your emotions; to activate unconditional love by awakening your spirit while ascending beyond the heavens.

When we think about our life and the journey ahead, there is nothing more important as what you imagine, what you dream yourself to be. It is not necessary to search for the definition of life in other people and the world's conditioning. Just be confident of your own gifts challenges and dreams. Life fortunes don't always end with results favorable to this earthly test. God has laid before us the purity of his heart allowing his spirit to flow mighty through us. The energy that is cloaked deep in the shadow of life holds our key to enlightenment. Discovering this universal peace creates within us inner joy that will unlock our spiritual nature. The seed of life is within each breath that we take uncovering God's power through the Holy Spirit. Without a greater understanding of our God Authority this human experience will be incomplete. May these words... Romance your Emotions and Spirit.

LOVE

Love has no limits...no time...no ending it
connects the heart mind and spirit.

Love hugs gently without pressure it
requires no conditions for giving love.

Love dreams thoughts of happiness hurt and
pain...deep and wide it's charity that fulfills our
mission the glue that binds seasons and time.

Love accepts me as I am; it's the
universal language of hope.

Love is the sound of leaves in the wind it's
the sight and smell of new birth.

Love has the aroma of a freshly cut hot apple
pie it's the glory and victory in the battle of
life the sunset that sets over a calm lake.

Love is the chill from a cold winter night it's warmth
that provides protection in a storm the shelter for our
inward peace it's our playground towards the future.

Love is fascinated with passion and appreciation
it delights in friendship with tenderness. Love
admires and captivates our innermost treasures...

"LOVE"

EZELLBLUES

A TALK WITH GOD

I had a talk with God one day about life's
ups and downs; he shared with me his
greatest love in Jesus Christ I found.

I had a talk with God one day about being
poor; he said to me my precious child just
walk through my heavenly door.

I had a talk with God one day about the
breath of life he gave; he said to me my
precious child within you I must prevail.

I had a talk with God one day about jealously
envy and strife; he said to me my precious
child they are all a part of life.

I had a talk with God one day about his
greatest sacrifice he said to me my precious
child you must stand up and fight.

I had a talk with God one day it seemed that he didn't
care he took away a love one it just didn't seem fair.

I had a talk with God one day about life and
about death he said to me my precious child
I have given you my best. LIFE and DEATH.

Then one day my God began to speak
to me and this is what he said.
Know the spirit that dwells within you; esteem others
better than yourself; know that I am a jealous God;
speak boldly my words to others; rejoice and pray daily
about eternal life; and love others unconditionally.

I had a talk with God that day and my spirit was
set free and now I can encourage you and you
and you just trust in him and you will see.

HER

My thoughts reveal visions of beauty galore as I waited
for that moment when she opened that door.

When she speaks the sound of her voice pleases
my heart that I made the right choice.

Her beauty passion and charm let's me know
that her spirit is soothing and warm.

The ideal man for her life will cause
her no envy jealously or strife.

Her love is strong, demanding and real; her
heart caring, open... gentle as steel.

Her life is young vibrant and just beginning;
the world is hers without and ending.

Her courage is in facing trials and tribulations; her
strength comes through God's power and evaluation.

Her challenges grows in leaps and bounds;
her joy is from within...warm and sound.

Her days are thoughtful full of giving; her heart...well... it keeps the needy living.

Her smile fills the room with cheer; her eyes are deep soft and clear.

Her glow helps you to see the light; her faith gives you strength to fight.

As she walks with amazing grace, the sun beams gently on her face. Her love endures for the human race... it's warm...it's gentle... it's full grace.

HER NAME IS:

"DESTINY"

WHO IS SHE

Who is she who brings life into this world
that nurtures and comforts her children
giving them hope for the future?

Who is she that possesses elegance and beauty that
holds the attention and willingness of all mankind?

Who is she that understands that life will
eventually uncover her true mission?

Who is she that can calm a broken heart while
uplifting and defending her own tribulations?

Who is she that drives the soul of man incompetent
and his spiritual manifestations inoperable?

Who is she whose voice dwells inward leaving an
echo that surrounds the foundation of our universe?

Who is she whose every motion creates anticipation
and strength that enables her to co-exists with man?

Who is she that men fight not only in their desire to
attract but, in their boldness to conquer her heart?

Who is she that her spirit defines the meaning of a
victorious woman standing boldly through life's journeys?

Who is she that longs for soft emotional conversations
with a man who has an emotional heart?

Who is she that no matter what her heart and spirit
gives her power and strength in living day to day?

Who is she that her soft movements flow
endlessly... onward...with power and beauty?

"WHO IS SHE"

TRAYVON MARTIN

You were loved by many the story of your
life opened and changed our hearts and
now it is time for us to play our part.

The path you walked while talking with a friend
was filled with joy and laughter from within.

You left home with a thirst and thoughts of candy
delight only to find yourself fighting for your life.

You stood your ground you fought the fight your
life gives meaning to the greater plight.

Your life was taken by evil thoughts filled with
hatred and jealously that has torn humanity apart.

Your family is grieving missing the sound
of your voice but they rejoice in knowing
that you are a part of God's heart.

Your memory will continue to define the meaning
of life with a greater purpose for us to fight.

EZELL BLUES 2019

HOME

A place where life begins where family is
defined and love is unconditional.

A place where God is the center of reference
and respect for others is real.

A place where trials and tribulations are
fought with faith and prayer.

A place where teamwork and service
brings organization and structure.

A place where communication and laughter
flourish through knowledge and truth.

A place where time and care combines
with hope and survival.

A place where the realities of life
creates the illusions of life.

A place where energy from the universe holds
the secrets to our total enlightenment... where
togetherness is the silent strength of oneness.

The design of life has placed unreal foundations that
keeps us from discovering our full potential as a FAMILY.

EZELL BLUES

EARLY MORNING EMOTIONS

What an enormous feeling that gives
birth to Early Morning Emotions.

The quietness and stillness allows your spirit
to flow and escape outside of self.

There is a peace that surrounds itself with the
Spirit that brings us one step closer to God.

As the early morning echoes with the sounds
of nature, the sun begins to shine softly the air
becomes brisk and the heart explodes with joy.

As the beginning of a new day creeps towards birth
life takes on a new understanding a new dimension.

This new birth evolved deep from within the
Spirit of man that connects flesh and blood
with God through the Holy Spirit.
To experience God is to celebrate his
awesome creation of the universe.

As we travel on this journey our emotions must reveal the essence of love... and radiate a peaceful joy that engulfs and enlightens our SPIRIT.

By discovering our true enlightenment... our true energy... we will unlock mysteries of the universe.

TRUE MOTIVES

Time has brought to our friendship hope, joy, love and
despair we have grown in life with a burning care.

Life is a battle with certain plans they will
develop as we begin to understand.

We never fully understood God's grace
neglecting our hearts and rightful place.

Our laughter seemed to have roots to grow as
our love and spirits had a special glow.

Our first kiss will always be memorable our
last touch will be just unforgettable.

I will never truly understand why for our
love you didn't take a chance.

I thought during the course of life you
fought and won the important fights.

Instead you let go without even delivering the first blow.

Even though there were conditions placed on our
love our lives seem to fit like a hand in a glove.

How can you bring closure to this book when
there are chapters you haven't even shook.

With space and time we have grown apart but
there is still love deep within my our hearts.

I write these thoughts with a heavy heart knowing
that you will always have a special part.

Never forget our special bond it's like a
quite breeze on an open pond.

Let's always keep open communication
just in case there are complications.

Our hearts must be reconcile to continue
life's journey with a smile.

As these words flow from my heart
I can be sure that I have played my part.

My prayer for us is this; to keep our
thoughts on God's special gifts.

EYES OF A CHILD

As we experience life through the eyes of a child
our thoughts develop and innocent style.

Their minds are beginning to envision life's character
not realizing the depths of their barriers.

As they continue to grow their courage
for life continues to show.

One door closes another door opens
their zest for life is always spoken.

As they develop that solid foundation their
love must evolve around God's creation.

How simple of an entrance into life God
took away all evil and strife.

Their eyes are the camera of their soul.
Their smile reflects their inward love.
Their tears may suggest a broken heart. The
words I love you may give it a spark.

As they strive for a greater understanding their scope
of life becomes more and more demanding.

Born into a world of the great unknown
beginning to live a life that is shown.

As a boy I grew in height and weight my
mind stumbled from all the freight.
My teenage years I developed sex appeal not
realizing what life was going to deal.

At twenty one I became a man not
realizing I needed a plan.

Thirty was a precious time living a
life that was totally divine.

At forty I became that prodigal son spending
my wealth on a whole lot of fun.

At forty-eight I barely escape a condition
of cancer from all my mistakes.

Through pain and suffering I called Him by name
he opened his arms and took away the pain.

EZELL BLUES

AT TIMES I STRUGGLE

I struggle during moments of soul discovering and
the desire to establish for myself foundations that
are critical to my overall existence. I struggle in
developing and monitoring human emotions.

I struggle with allowing life to just take it's course.

I struggle with believing that mankind
can no longer express LOVE.

I struggle with how man distorts the
truth of his power over the world.
"I STRUGGLE WITH THAT"

I struggle with knowing that life is not easy
knowing one day my body and soul will cease
my thoughts will no longer be my thoughts.

I struggle when I see poverty that exist around the world.

When I see that material things are more
important than eternal rewards.

When I see the tears of a child in need of love their
arms reaching out for protection and warmth.
"I STRUGGLE WITH THAT"

I struggle when I see our freedom and
liberties being attacked by our own system of
government, when I see man's quest for space
dominance causing global destruction.

I struggle knowing that we can not allow world
events to continue to have agendas whose
foundation is based on human suffering.
"I STRUGGLE WITH THAT"

I believe that the struggle in humankind will continue.
And as we struggle on this narrow road of life... our
lives gain spiritual birth leading to everlasting peace.

"I NO LONGER STRUGGLE WITH THAT"

EZELL BLUES

IMAGINE A WORLD

Imagine a world where the welfare of others came first in our lives where the color of our skin meant...nothing.

Imagine a world where the beauty of nature
is craved where our children are our future
where relationships are important.

Imagine a world where conversations dwell between the common man where the lost of innocent lives is not accepted where communities are protecting each other where the village was back raising our children.

Imagine a world where fathers stood up and
became fathers where mothers reverence
and respected their husbands.

"IMAGINE THAT WORLD"

Imagine a world where each of us will fulfill our purpose on earth where service to others is understood where our character is not based on others opinion of us where we hold on to the innocence of a child.

Imagine a world where war is avoided at all cost
where the environment was protected for the future
where the simple things brought the greatest pleasures
where homelessness is eliminated not nurtured
where we prayed daily for wisdom and knowledge.

Imagine a world where we truly loved
unconditionally where world leaders got together
and prayed where our differences are a plus where
God is the center of reference in our lives

"IMAGINE THAT WORLD"

EZELL BLUES

WHEN WE MEET

As I ponder what I might say when I first look into our
eyes, my heart will say... WOW what an incredible smile.

The first few moments might be a time of wondering;
wondering....does she like me wondering....
does he like me ... Ya know...she is sexy!!!

...And he is pleasing to the eyes!!!

What will we wear that might make
a statement of our character,

...something colorful yet
subtle ...something bold but warm

...something casual but sexy.

The wine I choose for the evening is refreshing
fruity and mild, candles are flickering creating
the essence of romance and sexuality.

As the evening slowly develops
...our conversation is warm

...our wine glasses are filled ...and love is in the air our lips touch gently arousing feelings deep from within.

As we embrace our passion explodes sounds
of satisfaction echoes between us

I need to hear and feel your ecstasy your passion your ultimate climax that will totally engulf my spirit.

Come with me while we penetrate with extreme passion
...the fiber of our hearts
...feeling the warmth of our love
...the emotions are intense
...our moment of fulfillment is near
...hold me close as we experience that moment! ! ! !

And now... we are one forever wanting and
needing that fulfillment...WHEN WE MEET.

THE RIVER-WALK

Here I am arriving at the River-walk
its early morning 6:00am
...the smell of beignets in the air coffee
and chicory please with cream.

The sound of Jazz fills the air
...boats traveling down the Mississippi
gracefully ...seagulls gliding overhead in search of prey.

Couples walking hand in hand with an occasional kiss.

The sound of waves on the banks of the Mississippi
...early morning fishermen catching their feast
...traffic moving slowly down Canal Street
...city sweepers on Bourbon Street

...St. Charles trolley full of passengers
in the Garden District.

The smell of red beans and rice with
smoke sausage...most be Monday.

Mardi Gras is in full swing with parades galore.

Fried catfish with jumbo shrimp
...low country boil with corn sausage and crabs.

The Saints win the Super Bowl...
the sights and sounds of New Orleans.

EZELL BLUES

OUR COMFORTABLE POSITION

Our passage in life has moved along a particular
course causing us to roam the streets searching
for direction longing for someone to listen...
to talk to...to hold... trying to find;
"Our comfortable position".

Nights are restless... lonely... hungry for some sort of
acknowledgment about what tomorrow will bring
to the day to day survival in this imperfect world...
that does not understand or know how to react to;
'Our comfortable position"

We all have different reasons for where we
are and how we feel so cozy...so sheltered...
so untroubled by; the environment, uncharted
surroundings, and circumstances that creates a
posture of uncertainty, that affect our thoughts and
behavior in this; "Our comfortable position".

The outlook in this uncomfortable position conjures
up feelings designed to nurture and prolong my
experience as I walk the street alone In this;
"Our comfortable Position"

Many seem to prosper from the misfortune of
many who struggle within themselves to process
a blueprint for their journey through life.

Earthly possessions controls most of our life.
Without those material things we crave their
presence, their convenience and status that does
not exist in this... "Our Uncomfonable Position".

Even though we have lingered within this illusion our
spirit screams loudly for a foundation that we might
understand the true vision of our calling in this;
"Our comfortable position"

EZELL BLUES

THE HEART BEAT OF LOVE

In my earthly walk my love will grow
stronger I will show the world through
Jesus Christ that love last longer.

I am an ordinary person filled with unconditional
love a love that flows like a heavenly dove.

How does love feel when it is given freely when
the giver understands the heart of the receiver.

When that love exist within our heart others
will discern that spiritual spark.

Our love has developed through the passing of
time as the sun continues to rise and shine.

With each thought our character grows stronger
giving us the strength to live our lives longer.

The world becomes our play ground of hope as we
look through the lens of the earth telescope.

The love we have is our inward glory each
moment gives grace to our whole life story.

Our love for humankind must be unconditional
and be not consumed by worldly traditions.

As the battle field grows larger and larger our
quest for love grows stronger and stronger.

My God!!!... perfect those things that pertains to
us give us your LOVE so there will be no fuss.

GOD'S GREAT LOVE

LOVE...DREAMS...TRUST...and HOPE
are what we need in order to cope.

To live our lives to the fullest length
God gives us his supernatural strength.

The days we are given are very small yet
life's journey must be strong and tall.

Life will hit us with many a blow but
God's great love helps us to grow.

As we travel within God's glory he
will reveal our own life story.

As babies we came into a world unknown in
God's great words our paths are shown.

Born with the spirit of Christ within our
faith gives us the strength to bend.

As we continue to study God's words our wisdom
and knowledge must be heard and as we pray day
by day it's in God's words that we must stay.

PAST-PRESENT-FUTURE

I remember not understanding the love of
God not knowing the sacrifice He made for
me not loving others unconditionally.

I remember living without God...without hope living on
the broad road of jealousy envy and the battle for life.

"1 REMEBER THE NIGHT... GOD
CHANGE MY LIFE"

I began to embrace the spirit within
embrace the love he has for all men.

I have embraced the goodness and joys of life.

I have embrace resentment greed and strife.

God's vision and hope for all man came in
Jesus Christ the sacrificial LAMB.

His vision was to teach all men how
to love and destroy all sin.

Our hearts are filled with the issues of life our
vision must include the lord Jesus Christ.

As we remember and consider our... "PAST"

While embracing and holding close to the... "PRESENT"

Let's envision the goal of eternity
in all of our... "FUTURE"

EZELLBLUES

PORTRAIT OF LOVE

Misty blue lights...glittering.. shinning
causing time to be filled with love.

The mellow sound of jazz piano piercing
the soul and the emotions within.

The look in your eyes and the smile on your
face tells me that romance is near.

Slowly we embrace triggering and
explosion buried deep in our hearts.

Kissing gently produces passion between us the
excitement of the moment is truly spectacular! ! !.

I step back looking at you feeling your
energy wanting your touch.

I adore the very ground you walk on even
that sparkle of confidence. Your heart
overwhelms and dazzles the imagination.

We are surrounded by all the comfort that life can
offer. Our world engulfs the foundation of Love.

Out commitment to grow to learn to
become as one help in our journey.

I still find myself wanting and needing to
be in your presence... in your arms.

Our laughter gives us hope for a brighter future.

Our spiritual growth has come with a
price knowing who we are in Christ.

With one accord with one voice we
have fought the battles of life.

Our hopes and dreams for our children
supersedes all of life...ETERNITY.

As we carry on this journey of life let's remember
that we are nothing more than spiritual
beings... living a human experience.

YOUR SMILE

Your smile sends... "a glimmer of hope to
every part of me" igniting the hymns of
nature and the seduction of life.

Your smile creates the mellow tone of living large in a
simpler place enhancing the smell and the color of spring.

Your smile dreams with excitement from the heart and...
"a glimmer of hope to every part of me."

Your smile is the characteristic of real love
the hope for survival helping overcome the
issues and realities in our way of life.

Your smile creates the afterglow of love and reveal
secrets from within surrounded by inspiration
motivation and the meaning of life.

Your smile encourage soul gathering and celebrates joyful
moments while dancing with an irresistible melody.

Your smile creates signs miracles and
wonders by rejoicing in delight and
"a glimmer of hope to every part of me."

Your smile shows phrase for the glory of God it brings comfort to those who are broken heart ed with no hope.

Your smile shows admiration and respect for the common man enduring many hardships many miracles.

Your smile answers all the question about knowing each other by our spirit and by adding

"A GLIMMER OF HOPE TO EVERY PART OF ME"

THERE COMES A TIME IN LIFE

There comes a time in life when our hearts
yearns for affection when we take a chance once
again to discover our spiritual connections.

When the walls of distrust comes tumbling down when
the course of our life builds courage that is sound.

When the pain in our life is replaced with joy when
we realize our hope is not a man made ploy.

When we walk out in faith each day as we pray when
we share God's words so that others might stay.

When the love for which we were made
continues to shine through fear when we take
note to witness how God loves us so dear.

When the goodness of man thirst for inward salvation
when the soul of man returns to it's natural creation.

Then and only then will the vividness
and quality of life be revealed by...

"ASCENDING"

Foster Parents Florence and Leslie Bell

Me and my twin sister.
Cozell Blues McCoil and Ezell Blues

My son Daniel D. Blues

DAY DREAMING

While listening to contemporary jazz
I am Day Dreaming about being I love.

Many times my heart has opened many
times closed not knowing real love.

I have often heard that in order to be with you
I have know you I don't even know myself so
for me to suggest knowing you...forget it.

I see this person as my soulmate my friend my
companion so many wonderful things will bring us
together they will give us a reason and a zest for life.

The foundation that will give us hope will
be our love and spiritual growth.

Even though we have not met our love grows stronger...
each day as I awake joyful thoughts collectively gather in
my heart your smile is etched on the projector of my soul.

There will be trials and tribulations during
our life but together we will fight.

Fulfilling our calling and passion for life
helps us to complete our battles in life.

Your strength courage and daring personality
is what I admire about you... your wisdom and
knowledge brings a moral fiber unmatched.

When we finally come together...and we will
many magnificent and glorious things will be
accomplished because of our commitment to share
unconditional love that flows like a quiet storm.

As I DAY DREAM this day each day my heart
radiates energy longing to be loved.

THE MANUAL OF LIF

I often wonder if I had a manual a book ʋ
instructions detailing my journey throu
life would it have made a difference?

Would this manual be so organized as to prec
my pains and joys moments of sorrow and haɪ

What about my spiritual belief would I h
a greater chance of knowing who God
will it teach me how to love others?

Would it enable me to be successful in my pro
career detailing all of mistakes...all of my prɩ

Will I stand a greater chance of knowir
how to raise my children?

Will it have stories about my parents and theiɪ
and their parents allowing me to understand ɪ

Will I have a greater understanding that peo
different and it's those differences that makes uɪ

Would I learn that the battle for life is within
each of us to explore and discover the truth
buried internally waiting to be loved?

Will it have a road map to the door steps of
heaven our passageway to eternity...will I be listed
in the book of life with all glory and honor?

Will I truly discover peace and quiet serenity that
will end hatred and poverty around the world?

Will this new world allow mankind to be what he was
born to be free and independent to roam this land
to live without hatred and jealously to love others
with the love of God in harmony with nature.

wished I had this manual when I came into this world

"THE MANUAL OF LIFE"

EZELL BLUES

PICTURE OF HOPE

The time:
dawning of a new day;

The setting:
early morning...cool...refreshing;

Talented minds:
gather to play the game of life;

Each surviving his own way in an unfriendly world.

Thoughts dominated by discontent... by sorrow.

Diverse cultures and beliefs...one race.

The main character... people; people who change
circumstances without changing themselves people
expecting more without a giving heart people whose
destination hampered by lack of love... lack of knowing
themselves spiritual... lacking willingness to change.

When life is threatened we cry for help...
We cry for another chance to make a difference...

Often our cry is in vain we treat life just the same.
Time is moving briskly vigorously waiting on
no one. Eventually time will come calling...
calling for a justification of life... was my
mission accomplished was the journey complete
were hearts healed and spirits revealed?

Was your life planned with eternity in mind...
was your heart truly truly divine.

STREET WALKERS

People in their own world strolling aimlessly
with no time...no purpose...no directions.

Stopping to talk to...no one there
Their cloth dressed in dirt
Shoes with no form
Their eyes expressmg inward pain
They stop momentarily searching
through rubbish.. for FOOD.

They come in many shapes and colors...
male and female young and old.
their days are never ending.

In their world there is no status...no class...no
structure their motivation... survival their shelter...the
elements of the earth their world...a lonely place.

Their friends are few...created in their own
thoughts it seems that life has stopped for
them their world has always been conditioned
their journey...thoughtless...empty

They thirst to be alone in their world...in their mind
their life...delusions filled with...uncertainty.

THEY AWAKE EARLY MORNING...
WALKING...WALKING...JUST WALKING.

EZELL BLUES

THE SOULFUL STRUT OF LIFE

As we dance The Soul Strut of Life...

Our strut is filtered with passion and irresistible
love reaching beyond and high into the heavens
resting deeply wanting tenderness.

Our strut is forever embedded in dreams and
hopes while dancing... "the soul strut of life".

Our strut exposes harmony and secrets resting inward
making music that excites and electrifies the spirit.

Our strut motivates and inspires greatness...
encourage poise...confidence and
self belief while dancing."
"the soul strut of life".

Our strut uncovers:
hardships suffering and sorrow building a fortress
filled with optimism and hopefulness.

Our strut discovers:
peace serenity and tranquility... in this reality.
Discerning love and hate constructs a solid foundation.

We must be:
expressive in thought:
vivid in imagination and dramatic in style
to create... "the soul strut of life".

THE NAKEDNESS OF GOD

We see Him as he is infinite intelligent
Spirit...pure...emotional....loving creator of
the heavens...master of the universe.

We feel His strength... His power...His supreme design
for all creation where galaxies baffle the imagination.

We see the greatness of His character in that He loved us
before the beginning of time before our very first breath.

We feel His enlightenment and vibrations by allowing His
spirit to roam in our hearts and in our foundation for life.

We feel His breath as the wind blows
north south east and west.

We see His love through the sacrifice
he made for on Calvary.

We long for His grace mercy and
peace during the time of need.

We crave the joy of His comforting arms
holding us... protecting the spirit.

We ponder His words of wisdom words
that express unconditional love.

We know that he wants us to be liked minded...
tenderhearted... forgiving one another.

We discover our nakedness from His wisdom
and knowledge that will cleanse the spirit.

We unfold the gift of Holy Spirit through
a relationship with Jesus Christ.

We glory in His honor rejoice in his
goodness and sing songs of phrase.

We heal naturally by having a positive attitude
and a constructive knowing of self.

We search high and low for answers of life
unwilling to compete on the narrow road of life.

When we surrender to God and lay before him
our hearts peace and tranquility multiplies.

God's intention for mankind has been distorted
into an illusion filled with earthly desires.

When we discover God's universal peace
within ourselves our thoughts are pruned
allowing our spirit to flow effortlessly.

THE ILLUMINATION

It was daybreak with the sun peaking over the horizon.

Breathing in captured in the freshness and
newness of the air the moment was surreal
encompassing all of nature...unbelievable.

Energy flowing incredibly amazingly
engulfing my whole being.

Closing my eyes feeling the power and authority
to ascend beyond the universe the energy grew
deeper...expanding my senses and feelings.

In an instant my whole body was
filled with PURE LOVE.

The weightlessness and radiance overflowing
with brightness and power.

My desire became oneness with God whose
light shines with sureness and dominance.

My quest is for the ultimate and supreme
relationship... in eternity.

The sun no loner was peaking but in
full sight packed with energy.

With my spirit facing the sun

I felt connected to all creations.

There was a quite softness with a gentle flow
of goodness uncovering PURE SELF.

Living in that present moment created
joy by discovering peace.

Self realization that validates this human experience
is a must in understanding our potential of activating
the consciousness beyond our current state... is real.

There is such a powerful energy waiting to
be unlocked that will open new frontiers in
your spirit and journey through life.

REFLECTIONS

Early one Sunday morning while fishing
the banks of the Mississippi

I glance upward experiencing the golden
splendors of our universe.. blue skies crisp
sunshine and the breeze of content.

As I sat listening to the sounds of nature my
soul became passionate while my spirit was set
free.. lingering in the essence are untold stories
miracles dreams and hopes of all mankind.

How often do we stop and reflect on the beauty
and magnitude of this universe in which we
live.. what ROLE do we play in the survival of
this vast phenomenon called the universe?

When we decide to embrace the fullness of life let's
consider our ROLE and understand that each day
is a dress rehearsal that will lead to the finale.

When that final curtain is drawn did we... stand
worthy of the many wonderful responsibilities as
we played our part did we... love with the same
love for which we were created and did we...
leave a legacy that will give glory to God?

And...it's still early Sunday morning and my thoughts
are torn between understanding what is my role...
my purpose what is my mission...my destiny?

I believe that we all have a mission in life together...
whether we live for God's purpose and allow his
plans to develop around us we must not disobey

His blueprints for our journey in life.

I dream often about a world where one day our survival
will be enhanced by helping others to survive.

I dream where the road of life creates obstacles designed
to allow us to stumble along the highway to eternity.

The twist and turn that we make in life reflects
the beauty and attitude on how we will embrace
life...and it's still early Sunday morning.

HI MOM

On this extraordinary day there are many
unique reasons for loving you.

You carried me next to your heart for many months while
experiencing many hours of pain while giving me birth.

You gave me your milk and substance
of life as you nurtured me.

You stared at me often looking intently
wondering my future.

You dressed me with warm comfortable colors and
taught me how to count and know my ABC's.

You demanded a Godly understanding
of my spiritual nature.

You cried when I hurt and laughed during moments of joy.

You showed me how to love without conditions
you uplifted my accomplishments and comforted
me during stress your tears watered my heart
while exposing and revealing my love.

Your smile has changed many lives
and warmed many hearts.

Your generosity charity and harmony
bring peace in a storm.

Your happiness and exhilaration for life
gives others hope and faith in life.

I may have never told you this but,

I am glad God selected you as my mother.

You are the most wonderful mother in the world.

My love and respect for you grows stronger each day.

Always remember that you are special to me to my
life on this day and everyday for the rest of our lives.

"1 LOVE YOU MOM"

PSSST

Pssst... hey there... I thought that I might
interest you in a conversation.

You don't really know who I am but

I have been apart of you for a longtime we came into this
world together as one... I am buried deep within you.

You give more time to your outward manifestation
forgetting about me... spending your days chasing the
American Dream... nice car... big house... three kids.

My passion...my dream...my gladness is
for us to get to know one another.

1 AM YOUR SPIRIT..PSST...are you still listening?

A man by the name of Jesus Christ died...

I am that spirit of God in Christ in you...

I am the glue your life line to heaven
the way the truth and the light.

I am the voice of God wanting to help you on your journey to eternity. I have waited for you to recognize my thoughts my wisdom...my tenderness.

I dream of a personal relationship with you that is overflowing with love. Turn on that light and allow me to grow in you spiritually.

I will teach you to speak with other tongues the wonderful works of God.

Your heart is one of giving blessing and esteeming others better than yourself. There were times when I thought I had your attention only to realize... I did not.

Why do I pierce your heart because I am responsible for our salvation.

Together we will complete God's mission for us on earth. One other thing before I go...

our journey will be gone in the blank of an eye.

So let's prepare ourselves with that breast plate of righteousness and that helmet of salvation.

Together we are one... PSSST...are you still listening

OUR WHISPERS

Whispers proclaim secrets that are softly spoken
with a distinctive rhythm...musically expressive.

Relax with whispers that anticipate passion
infatuations... and the fascinations of our dreams.

Adore and worship everyday that creates our
journey through life... with a whisper.

Be in love with whispering at mornings filled
with excitement and admiration for life giving
respect for the effortless passage in life.

Be devoted to listening to the softer side of a whisper
that mutter words of coziness words of relaxation.

Be hopeful look forward to predict and scrutinize
those whispers coming from our hearts.

We often ignore and turn our back on whispers that
challenge our preparation for living in eternity.

Cherish and reverence the natural seasons of life
as we whisper the wonderful works of GOD.

In the end were our whispers loud enough
did they possess power for those to hear.

AWAKE!!! feeling each day as a new beginning with
fresh new whispers...telling us to smile and feel the
spirit of joy in ourselves and others... "our whispers".

A young man that I am mentoring called me one day and ask me to give his girlfriend's dad a call. He had been diagnosed with a deadly form of cancer and was given three days to live. He also mentioned that he wasn't responding to anyone he was not coherent. I thought to myself...if he is not responding to anyone how could I make a difference. I told him to give his girlfriend my telephone number. The next day I received a call from her while she was at the hospital with her dad. I spoke with her for a few minutes introducing myself to her. After getting to know her I asked her what was happening with her father, she stated that his conditioned had not changed that he was still not responding to anyone are anything. Again I am thinking how can I make a difference by talking with him. She said... I can put the telephone to his ear and you can talk with him. I asked her what is his name? She said John David...I said OK. So she put the telephone to his ear and I said good morning John David in my most cheerful voice. At that moment he screamed at the top of his voice saying that my voice sent fire from the top of his head through his entire body. He became coherent and responsive. The nurses came running in the room to see what was happening. I felt the excitement of everyone even though I wasn't physically there. At that moment I realize that I was a vessel of God's healing. That experience has truly humble my emotions to where I have become this empathetic being searching to love purely.

My story began My 30th 1956 born in Norco, Louisiana with my twin sister Cozell into a life filled with God's healing presence. When we were eighteen months old most of the children that my mother had were taken from her and were all placed in foster homes because of neglect. The story goes as follows. One night while leaving the children alone she went dancing. That night a rat came into the house and was able in get into the crib and bit into one of the other twins that were only about nine months old. Because of that incident the welfare system came and placed us in different foster homes. If we had remained in that environment being neglected... I would have died. The twins were kept together. Cozell and I were placed in the home of Mr. and Ms. Leslie Bell in Gramercy Louisiana. I was in such bad shape when I arrived they were told to take care of the little girl (Cozell) the boy want be here that long. They were a blessing from God as they knew how to heal me from all the worms and other things going on in my eighteen month old body.

At age fourteen I made an attempt to get to know my earthly mother. So I packed a suitcase to go visit her. Upon my arrival at the bus station I expected to see her there instead she sent the neighbor to pick me up. When I finally arrived to her house the first thing she said to me was this... "you think you are better than people by the way you dress". I did not know how to respond to that comment. She had not seem me since I was eighteen months old now I am fourteen. That statement sent such an empty feeling in my heart. I did not feel loved or even wanted. I packed enough clothing to last a week. Because of how I was being treated I awoke the next day and asked to be taken to the bus station. She said it would be her pleasure. I knew then that she was not interested in loving or getting to know me.

My foster parents were simple folks who were God sent to Cozell and I to become a part of their family. They had two children of their own before we came aboard. They were entrepreneur in that they purchased two homes moved them onto their property and rented them out to folks in the neighborhood. As a young kid he taught me the love of fishing and believe me it was the most exciting thing to do as a young child. I was very shy as a young boy with with unknown potential growing within me. At the age of seven a music teacher who visited my elementary school was interested in actually adopting me into her family. She was a white woman who wanted to train me in music and other facet of my life. There was something that she saw in me that she wanted to develop and nurture. Of course my foster parents would not split up Cozell and I. Later in life I reflected on that moment sometimes wondering... what if. I had the ability to memorize almost anything I put my hands on starting with, "IT Was The Night before Christmas" in one and half days. I will share my full life story in my next book entitled, "A Vessel of God's Love".

MOTOVATING THOUGHTS OF LOVE

"Love sought is good, but given unsought
is better". —Shakespeare

"Love looks not with the eyes, but with
the mind". —Shakespeare

''Love which is only an episode in the life of a man, is
the entire history of a woman's life". —Mad DE Stael

"The heart of him who truly Loves is a paradise on earth,
he has God in himself, for God is Love". Lameness

"Love is an image of God, and not a lifeless
image, but the living essence of the divine nature
which beams full of goodness". —Luther

"Love gives itself; it is not bought". —Longfellow

"Where Love and wisdom drink out of the same cup, in
this every-day world, it is the exception". —Mad Necker

"Life is a flower of which Love is
the honey". —Victor Hugo

"To Love is to place your happiness in the
happiness of others". —Leibnitz

OUR EMOTIONS

Our emotions directs the energy that exist
deep in the morsel of our soul.

Our emotions nurtures our thoughts
giving us the ability to envision life.

Our emotions causes joy and suffering.

Our emotions generates selfish desires aimed at total
physical enunciation of our inward substance.

Our emotions grows daily from wisdom and
knowledge gained by the process of life.

Our emotions rise and fall with time leaving open the
road to hope that helps us to understand and discern
spiritual manifestations through hearing God's voice.

Our emotions should challenge the essence of
our existence through daily evaluations.

Our emotions are pruned as we walk in faith and
courage knowing eternal rewards are gathered.

Our emotions are part of our total experiences of life,
that gives birth to feelings that dwell through us.

HAPPINESS

Happiness finds pleasure in the softness of a new
day the dawning of night, it delights in charm
while creating a keen fondness for joy.

Happiness respects and esteem others better
than oneself and having he willingness to
allow your heart to be pruned...by GOD.

Happiness establishes and determines some of
life's greatest wonders, like the smile and look on
an infant's face while exploring their world.

Happiness is being able to confront and know
the person in the mirror, being honest about
your ups and downs...your ins and outs.

Happiness is God working on the outside, a fragrance we
love to smell, a breeze that blows softly across still waters.

Happiness is the enjoyment of watching nature in the
early dew, the hurt and pain that comes with existing.

Happiness is the moving force and driving energy of everyday life, can cause joyfulness with ecstasy and bliss.

Happiness masterfully designs and suggest our thoughts, is dependent upon one another for surviving this changing world.

Happiness is to truly know who we are in the Spirit, happiness is JOY turned inside out.

EZELL BLUES

HI DAD

On this special occasion I would like to reflect
on the role that you have played in my life.

You started by fertilizing the egg that created me.

You had moming sickness during moms nine months.

You brought me to my first six weeks check up.

You had tears watching while I slept...
dreaming of my future.

You worked hard providing a home and security for
the family, your talent for cooking is appreciated.

Your love for the outdoors rubbed off
on everyone... especially fishing.

You planted gardens that grew out of this world vegetables.

Your guidance and discipline helped
build a foundation to grow.

Your tenderness and love for mom shows in your smile.

So often in life we acquire many identities that form and shape our flesh and blood experience.

As I have grown into adulthood I see a lot of you in me.

My zest for life comes from the love that you continue to show for me... 1 LOVE YOU DAD.

THE COLOR OF LOVE

The color of love is a feeling of affection.... it's a
gentle touch that we are passionate about... the
emotional and tender style in which we love.

We fall in love for many reasons...many intentions.

So often in life we love for the wrong reasons...
wrong purpose not knowing the true color of love.

Imagine if the color love had no meaning...
no implications of worth how would
we know that we are in love.

Why is love so important to this human experience?
Why is there a need within us to be in love?
What is the objective of being in love?

The bible says that "God is Love" and
in him there is no darkness at all.

The color of love is light...created in the image
of God we know that love starts in the heart
the fundamental makeup of who we are.

The spirit of God that is in each of us...is love.

Love is also the many feelings and obsessions
we have buried deep within us.

Being passionate about self enables and
produces love from the heart.

The Color of LOVE sets in motion and activates
the spirit of God's light in our hearts.

TEARDROP

It's from those unusual feelings within
us that A Teardrop is born.

The more we reflect on those feelings A Teardrop
becomes an... uncontrollable stream of emotions.

A Teardrop starts with watery eyes and
a feeling that touches the heart.

It moves softly, cautiously.. resting on the
chin filled with emotions of joy or pain.

Bringing new life into the world; the lost of love ones;
the thrill of succeeding, all may cause A Teardrop...

Upon our arrival in the world the first thing
we do is produce A Teardrop...we cry.

Tears for a man is a must, it creates within him the
sensitive nature of God and the ability to feel others.

The man who is not emotional enough to show tears
is losing the battle in understanding himself.

God in all of his magnificent glory also has
feelings, those of tears, love, mercy and grace
in order that he might know mankind.

Whenever the urge to cry is upon you...

allow it to become visible and relieve the
emotions surrounding it... "A TEARDROP"

MY DEAREST SARAH

The night was young and our emotions
reached beyond the heavens

Onto a planet filled with the gentle softness
of hope love and the wonders of eternity.

As we gently touch the look of love
comes streaming from our hearts.

Remember the way we were how love and
passion guided our journey how our love
transformed and healed our spirits.

As we travel on this new planet the early
morning echoes with the sounds of peace...a
peace that brings us closer to God.

As the beginning of a new day creeps toward birth,
life takes on a new dimension a new blessing.

The quietness and stillness allows
the spirit to flow effortlessly.

This new birth evolves deep from within the spirit of man that connects flesh and blood with God through the Holy Spirit.

EZELL BLUES

MESSAGE FROM EARTH

Hey!!! before you leave today for work I wonder
if I may have a word with you something
very important we must discuss.

We need to talk about my expectation
for surviving the future.

Yes, I was created with you in mind a place where
natural beauty was designed for your existence.

Where waters gracefully flow bringing endless comfort
and a sun that provides warmth and affection.

Where valleys and oceans rule supreme and natural
energy floats elegantly over my massive body.

I have rainbows and tropical storms that are far
reaching and all embracing that completes my life.

My cloud cover skies provide relief from the sun
where lakes and rivers are pure and bountiful.

My ice covered mountaintops reach to the heavens.

But what I am feeling is uncertainty... I will tell you why.

I am more than just dirt, I am alive filled
with power and might. I am where plants
grow and where we live in search of life.

I leave you with this one thought;

Mankind must begin to address how he lives
in order that I might have a future.

"I am the Earth"

INNER MAN

OK, I know that you received a Message
from Earth and your Spirit Pssst at you.

I was wondering if I might have a minute of your
time. Let me take this moment to introduce myself.

I am the other part of your Spirit, that
soul and intellectual part of you.

I open your eyes to those personal moments,
hose internal and private feelings.

You might say that I have a soft voice whispering
words of comfort protecting the heart and
mind giving advice on issues of life.

1 AM YOUR INNER MAN, longing for recognition.

I watch you everyday put on the mask
of life hiding our true essence.

Truly more preparation is given to
your worldly appearance.

Let me explain in a sampler way...

I need you, I need you...and I love you.

If you take the time to say hello

I promise an honest chat. The key word is... HONEST.

Let's get honest and figure out what our experience is truly about how do we compete in the challenges of life.

I know there are many things hidden mysteriously that are unsolved and unexplained about the course of our life.

The magnificent thing about our hope is that

God has given us of his glorious spirit
with a grand design for eternal life.

My fundamental nature gives real meaning
in defining the core of our heart projecting
empathy with a whole lot of tenderness.

These few minutes has given me confidence
that you will make an attempt to share the
rest of your life growing in the spirit.

I want you to always remember that

I will never leave you or forsake you...I am

Printed in the United States
By Bookmasters